Rush Benjamin

Considerations on the Injustice and Impolicy of Punishing

Murder by Death

Rush Benjamin

Considerations on the Injustice and Impolicy of Punishing Murder by Death

ISBN/EAN: 9783337149888

Printed in Europe, USA, Canada, Australia, Japan

Cover: Foto ©ninafisch / pixelio.de

More available books at **www.hansebooks.com**

CONSIDERATIONS

ON THE

INJUSTICE AND IMPOLICY

OF

PUNISHING MURDER BY DEATH.

EXTRACTED FROM THE

AMERICAN MUSEUM.

WITH ADDITIONS.

By BENJAMIN RUSH, M. D.

PROFESSOR OF THE INSTITUTES, AND OF CLINICAL MEDICINE,

IN THE UNIVERSITY OF PENNSYLVANIA.

PHILADELPHIA:

FROM THE PRESS OF MATHEW CAREY.

MAY 4—M,DCC,XCII.

CONSIDERATIONS, &c.

IN an essay upon the effects of public punishments upon criminals and upon society, published in the second volume of the American Museum, I hinted, in a short paragraph, at the injustice of punishing murder by death. I shall attempt in the following essay, to support that opinion, and to answer all the objections that have been urged against it.

I. Every man possesses an absolute power over his own liberty and property, but not over his own life. When he becomes a member of political society, he commits the disposal of his liberty and property to his fellow citizens; but as he has no right to dispose of his life, he cannot commit the power over it to any body of men. To take away life, therefore, for any crime, is a violation of the first political compact.

II. The punishment of murder by death, is contrary to reason, and to the order and happiness of society.

1. It lessens the horror of taking away human life, and thereby tends to multiply murders.

2. It produces murder, by its influence upon people who are tired of life, and who, from a supposition, that murder is a less crime than suicide, destroy a life (and often that of a near connexion) and afterwards deliver themselves up to justice, that they may escape from their misery by means of a halter.

3. The punishment of murder by death, multiplies murders, from the difficulty it creates of convicting persons who are guilty of it. Humanity, revolting at the idea of the severity and certainty of a capital punishment, often

fteps in, and collects fuch evidence in favour of a murderer, as fcreens him from juftice altogether, or palliates his
crime into manflaughter. If the punifhment of murder
confifted in long confinement, and hard labour, it would be
proportioned to the meafure of our feelings of juftice, and
every member of fociety would be a watchman or a magiftrate, to apprehend a deftroyer of human life, and to bring
him to punifhment.

4. The punifhment of murder by death, checks the operations of univerfal juftice, by preventing the punifhment
of every fpecies of murder. Quack doctors—frauds of va-
rious kinds—and a licentious prefs, often deftroy life, and
fometimes with malice of the moft propenfe nature. If
murder were punifhed by confinement and hard labour, the
authors of the numerous murders that have been mentioned, would be dragged forth, and punifhed according to
their deferts. How much order and happinefs would arife
to fociety from fuch a change in human affairs! But who
will attempt to define thefe fpecies of murder, or to pro-
fecute offenders of this ftamp, if death is to be the punifhment of the crime after it is admitted, and proved to be
wilful murder?—only alter the punifhment of murder, and
thefe crimes will foon affume their proper names, and probably foon become as rare as murder from common acts of
violence.

5. The punifhment of murder by death, has been proved
to be contrary to the order and happinefs of fociety by the
experiments of fome of the wifeft legiflators in Europe.
The emprefs of Ruffia, the king of Sweden, and the duke
of Tufcany, have nearly extirpated murder from their do-
minions, by converting its punifhment into the means
of benefiting fociety, and reforming the criminals who per-
petrate it.

III. The punifhment of murder by death, is contrary to
divine revelation. A religion which commands us to forgive
and even to do good to our enemies, can never authorife
the punifhment of murder by death. "Vengeance is mine,"
faid the Lord; "I will repay." It is to no purpofe to fay
here, that this vengeance is taken out of the hands of an individual, and directed againft the criminal by the hand of
government. It is equally an ufurpation of the prerogative
of heaven, whether it be inflicted by a fingle perfon, or by
a whole community.

Here I expect to meet with an appeal from the letter and
fpirit of the gofpel, to the law of Mofes, which declares,
that "he that killeth a man fhall furely be put to death."

Forgive, indulgent heaven ! the ignorance and cruelty of man, which by the misapplication of this text of scripture, has so long and so often stained the religion of Jesus Christ with folly and revenge.

The following considerations, I hope, will prove that no argument can be deduced from this law, to justify the punishment of murder by death. On the contrary, that several arguments against it, may be derived from a just and rational explanation of that part of the levitical institutions.

1. There are many things in scripture *above*, but nothing *contrary* to reason. Now, the punishment of murder by death, is *contrary* to reason. It cannot, therefore, be agreeable to the will of God.

2. The order and happiness of society cannot fail of being agreeable to the will of God. But the punishment of murder by death, destroys the order and happiness of society. It must therefore be contrary to the will of God.

3. Many of the laws given by Moses, were accommodated to the ignorance, wickedness, and " hardness of heart" of the Jews. Hence their divine legislator expressly says, " I gave them statutes that were *not good*, and judgments whereby *they should not live*." Of this, the law which respects divorces, and the law of retaliation, which required " an eye for an eye, and a tooth for a tooth," are remarkable instances.

But we are told, that the punishment of murder by death, is founded not only on the law of Moses, but upon a positive precept given to Noah and his posterity, that " whoso sheddeth man's blood, by man shall his blood be shed." In order to show that this text does not militate against my proposition, I shall beg leave to transcribe a passage from an essay on crimes and punishments, published by the reverend mr. Turner, in the second volume of the Manchester memoirs. " I hope," says this ingenious author, " that I shall not offend any one, by taking the liberty to put my own sense upon this celebrated passage, and to enquire, why it should be deemed a precept at all. To me, I confess, it appears to contain nothing more than a declaration of what will generally happen ; and in this view, to stand exactly upon the same ground with such passages as the following : " He that leadeth into captivity shall go into captivity." " He that taketh up the sword, shall perish by the sword*."—The form of expression is exactly the same in

* Rev. xv, 10.

each of the texts; why, then, may they not all be inter-preted in the same manner, and confidered, not as com-mands, but as denunciations? and if fo, the magiftrate will be no more bound by the text in Genefis, to punifh murder with death, than he will by the text in the Revelations, to fell every Guinea captain to our Weft India planters; and yet, however juft and proper fuch a proceeding might be, I fuppofe no one will affert that the magiftrate is bound to it by that, or any other text in the fcriptures, or that that alone would be admitted as a fufficient reafon for fo extraordinary a meafure.'

If this explanation of the precept given to Noah, be not fatisfactory, I fhall mention another. Soon after the flood, the infancy and weaknefs of fociety rendered it impoffible to punifh murder by *confinement*. There was therefore no medium between inflicting death upon a murderer, and fuf-fering him to efcape with impunity, and thereby to perpe-trate more acts of violence againft his fellow creatures. It pleafed God in this condition of the world to permit a *lefs* in order to prevent a *greater* evil. He therefore commits *for a while* his exclufive power over human life, to his creatures for the fafety and prefervation of an infant fociety, which might otherwife have perifhed, and with it, the only ftock of the human race. The command indirectly implies that the crime of murder was not punifhed by death in the ma-ture ftate of fociety which exifted before the flood. Nor is this the only inftance upon record in the fcriptures in which God has delegated his power over human life to his creatures. Abraham expreffes no furprife at the command which God gave him to facrifice his fon. He fubmits to it as a precept founded in reafon and natural juftice, for nothing could be more obvious than that the giver of life had a right to claim it *when* and in *fuch manner* as he pleafed. 'Till men are able to give life, it becomes them to tremble at the thought of *taking it* away. Will a man rob God?—Yes —he robs him of what is infinitely dear to him—of his darling attribute of *mercy*, every time he deprives a fellow creature of life.

4. If the Mofaic law with refpect to murder, be obligato-ry upon chriftians, it follows that it is equally obligatory upon them to punifh adultery, blafphemy, and other capital crimes that are mentioned in the levitical law, by death. Nor is this all: it juftifies the extirpation of the Indians, and the enflaving of the Africans; for the command to the Jews to deftroy the Canaanites, and to make flaves of their heathen neighbours, is as pofitive as the command which

declares, " that he that killeth a man, shall surely be put to death."

5. Every part of the levitical law, is full of types of the Messiah. May not the punishment of death, inflicted by it, be intended to represent the demerit and consequences of sin, as the cities of refuge were the offices of the Messiah ?

6. The imperfection and severity of these laws were probably intended farther—to illustrate the perfection and mildness of the gospel dispensation. It is in this manner that God has manifested himself in many of his acts. He created darkness first, to illustrate by comparison the beauty of light; and he permits sin, misery, and death in the moral world, that he may hereafter display more illustriously the transcendent glories of righteousness, happiness, and immortal life. This opinion is favoured by St. Paul, who says, " the law made nothing perfect," and that " it was a shadow of good things to come."

How delightful to discover such an exact harmony between the dictates of reason, the order and happiness of society, and the precepts of the gospel ! There is a perfect unity in truth. Upon all subjects—in all ages—and in all countries—truths of every kind agree with each other.

It has been said, that the common sense of all nations, and particularly of savages, is in favour of punishing murder by death.

The common sense of all nations is in favour of the commerce and slavery of their fellow creatures. But this does not take away from their immorality. Could it be proved that the Indians punish murder by death, it would not establish the right of man over the life of a fellow creature, for revenge we know in its utmost extent is the universal and darling passion of all savage nations. The practice moreover, (if it exist) must have originated in *necessity;* for a people who have no settled place of residence, and who are averse from all labour, could restrain murder in no other way. But I am disposed to doubt whether the Indians punish murder by death among their own tribes. In all those cases where a life is taken away by an Indian of a *foreign* tribe, they always demand the satisfaction of *life* for *life.* But this practice is founded on a desire of preserving a balance in their numbers and power ; for among nations which consist of only a few warriors, the loss of an individual often destroys this balance, and thereby exposes them to war or extermination. It is for the same purpose of keeping up an equality in numbers and power, that they often adopt captive children into their nations and families. What makes this explanation of the practice of punishing murder by death among the Indians more probable, is, that we find the same bloody and vindictive satisfaction is required for a foreign nation, whether the person lost, be killed by an accident, or by premeditated violence. Many facts might be mentioned from travellers to prove that the Indians do not punish murder by death within the jurisdiction of their own tribes. I shall mention only one which is taken from the rev. mr. John Megapolensis's account of the Mohawk Indians, lately published in mr. Hazard's historical collection of state papers.—" There is no punishment, (says our author) here for murder, but every one is his own avenger. The friends of the deceased revenge themselves upon the murderer until peace is made with the next akin. But although they are so cruel, yet there are not half so many murders committed among them as among christians, notwithstanding their severe laws, and heavy penalties."

It has been said, that the horrors of a guilty conscience proclaim the justice and necessity of death, as a punishment for murder. I draw an argument of another nature from this fact. Are the horrors of conscience the punishment that God inflicts upon murder? why, then, should we shorten or destroy them by death, especially as we are taught to direct the most atrocious murderers to expect pardon in the future world? no, let us not counteract the government of God in the human breast: let the murderer live—but let it be to suffer the reproaches of a guilty conscience: let him live, to make compensation to society for the injury he has done it, by robbing it of a citizen: let him live to maintain the family of the man whom he has murdered: let him live, that the punishment of his crime may become universal: and lastly let him live—that murder may be extirpated from the list of human crimes!

Let us examine the conduct of the moral Ruler of the world towards the first murderer: see Cain returning from his field, with his hands reeking with the blood of his brother! Do the heavens gather blackness, and does a flash of lightning blast him to the earth? no. Does his father Adam, the natural legislator and judge of the world, inflict upon him the punishment of death?—No; the infinitely wise God becomes his judge and executioner. He expels him from the society of which he was a member. He fixes in his conscience a never-dying worm. He subjects him to the necessity of labour; and to secure a duration of his punishment, proportioned to his crime, he puts a mark or prohibition upon him, to prevent his being put to death, by weak and angry men; declaring, at the fame time, that " whofoever flayeth Cain, vengeance fhall be taken on him feven-fold."

Judges, attornies, witneffes, juries and fheriffs, whofe office it is to punifh murder by death, I befeech you to paufe, and liften to the voice of reafon and religion, before you convict or execute another fellow-creature for murder!

But I defpair of making fuch an impreffion upon the prefent citizens of the united ftates, as fhall abolifh the abfurd and unchriftian practice. From the connexion of this effay with the valuable documents of the late revolution contained in the American Mufeum, it will probably defcend to pofterity. To you, therefore, the unborn generations of the next century, I confecrate this humble tribute to juftice. You will enjoy in point of knowledge, the meridian of a day, of which we only perceive the twilight. You will often review with equal contempt and horror, the indolence, ignorance and cruelty of your anceftors. The groffeft crimes fhall not exclude the perpetrators of them from your pity. You will *fully* comprehend the extent of the difcoveries and precepts of the gofpel, and you will be actuated, I hope, by its gentle and forgiving fpirit. You will fee many modern opinions in religion and government turned upfide downwards, and many new connexions eftablifhed between caufe and effect. From the importance and deftiny of every human foul, you will acquire new ideas of the dignity of human nature, and of the infinite value of every act of benevolence that has for its object, the bodies, the fouls, and the lives of your fellow-creatures. You will love the whole human race, for you will perceive that you have a common Father, and you will learn to imitate him by converting thofe punifhments to which their folly or wickednefs have expofed them, into the means of their reformation and happinefs.

*SOON after the above enquiry was published in the American
Museum, a reply to it made its appearance in the Pennsylvania Mercury, under the signature of* Philochoras ; *which produced the following answer. The principal arguments in favour of punishing murder by death, contained in the reply, are
mentioned in the answer, for which reason it was not thought
necessary to re-publish the whole of the reply in the order in
which it appeared in the news paper.*

FROM THE AMERICAN MUSEUM.

Mr. Carey,

I HAVE read a reply subscribed Philochoras, to an enquiry into the justice and policy of punishing murder by
death, published some time ago in the Museum. The author
of it has attempted to justify public and capital punishments,
as well as war, by the precepts of the gospel.—Let not
my readers suppose that this author is a sceptic—or a heathen—or that he is in any degree unfriendly to christiani-
ty. Far from it—he is a minister of the gospel—and a man
of a worthy private as well as public character.

Our author begins his reply by asserting, that the objection to the punishment of death for murder, proceeded ori-
ginally from the socinian objection to the great doctrine of
the atonement. Here I must acknowledge my obligations to
our author for having furnished me with a new argument in
favour of my principles. I believe in the doctrine of the
atonement, not only because it is clearly revealed in the
old and new testaments, but because it is agreeable to nature, and reason. Life is the product of death, through-
out every part of the animal creation. Reason likewise es-
tablishes the necessity of the atonement, for it has lately
taught us in the writings of the marquis of Beccaria,
that in a perfect human government there should be
no pardoning power: and experience has taught us that
where *certainty* has taken the place of *severity* of punishment, crimes have evidently and rapidly diminished
in every country. The demands of the divine law which
made the shedding of blood necessary to the remission
of sin, is a sublime illustration of the perfection of the
divine government, and of the love of the Supreme
Being to his intelligent creatures. But in the demand
of life for disobedience, let the divine law stand alone.
Men stand in a very different relation to each other, from

that which God fuftains to men. They are all falli-
ble, and deficient in a thoufand duties which they owe
to each other. They are bound, therefore, by the precept of doing to others, as they would have them do them,
to *forgive*, without a fatisfaction, inafmuch as they con-
ftantly require the fame *forgivenefs* to be exercifed towards
themfelves. To punifh murder, therefore, or any other
crime, by death, under the gofpel difpenfation, is to exalt
the angry and vindictive paffions of men to an equality
with the perfect law of God. It is to place imperfect individuals and corrupted human governments, upon the throne
of the righteous judge of the univerfe : nay, more—it is to
make the death of Chrift of no effect ; for every time we
punifh murder by death, we practically deny that it was a
full expiation for every fin, and thereby exclude ourfelves
from deriving any benefit from it, for he has made the forgivenefs of injuries, without any exceptions, whether committed againft us in our private capacities, or as members of
a community, the *exprefs condition* of our title to the forgivenefs which he has purchafed for us by his death.　　　・

The arguments againft the punifhment of murder by
death, from *reafon*, remain on an immoveable foundation.
Our author has *contradicted*—but has not *refuted* one of
them. I affirmed in my former effay, that the punifhment
of murder by death had been abolifhed in feveral of the
European nations. I wifh for the honour of our author's
profeffion, he had doubted of this affertion with more of
the meek and gentle fpirit of a chriftian. To fatisfy him
upon this fubject, I fhall fubjoin the following extracts from
authorities which are now before me.—In the inftructions
to the commiffioners appointed to frame a new code of
laws for the Ruffian empire, by Catharine II. the prefent
emprefs of Ruffia, I find the following paffage. I take great
pleafure in tranfcribing it, as the fentiments it contains
do fo much honour not only to the female underftanding,
but to the human mind.

" Proofs from facts demonftrate to us, that the frequent
ufe of capital punifhments, never mended the morals of a
people. Therefore, if I prove the death of a citizen to be
neither *ufeful* nor *neceffary* to fociety in general, I fhall con-
fute thofe who rife up againft humanity. In a reign of
peace and tranquillity, under a government eftablifhed with
the united wifhes of a whole people, in a ftate well fortifi-
ed againft external enemies, and protected within by ftrong
fupports ; that is, by its own internal ftrength, and virtu-
ous fentiments, rooted in the minds of the citizens, there

man be *no necessity* for *taking away the life* of a citizen. It is not the *excess* of severity, nor the *destruction* of the human species, that produces a powerful effect upon the hearts of the citizens, but the *continued duration* of the punishment. The death of a malefactor is not so efficacious a method of deterring from wickedness, as the example continually remaining, of a man who is deprived of his liberty, that he might repair, during a life of labour, the injury he has done to the community. The terror of death excited by the imagination may be more *strong*, but has not force enough to resist that *oblivion* which is so natural to mankind. It is a general rule, that rapid and violent impressions upon the human mind, disturb and *give pain*, but do not operate long upon the *memory*. That a punishment, therefore, might be conformable with justice, it ought to have such a degree of severity as might be sufficient to deter people from committing the crime. Hence I presume to affirm, that there is no man who, upon the least degree of reflexion, would put the *greatest possible* advantages, he might flatter himself from a crime, on the *one side*, into the balance against a life *protracted* under a *total* privation of liberty, *on the other*."

In a British review for the present year, I find a short account of the code of penal laws lately enacted by the emperor of Germany. This enlightened monarch has divided imprisonment into *mild—severe—*and *rigorous*. For the crime of murder, he inflicts the punishment of rigorous imprisonment—which from its duration, and other terrifying circumstances that attend it, is calculated to produce more beneficial effects in preventing murders, than all the executions that have ever taken place in any age or country.

I derived my information of the abolition of capital punishment in Sweden and Tuscany, from two foreigners of distinction, who lately visited the united states. The one was an Italian nobleman, the other was a captain in the Swedish navy—both of whom commanded every where respect and attachment for their abilities and virtues.

It is true, this happy revolution in favour of justice and humanity, in the instances that have been mentioned, did not originate in a convocation or a synod. It may either be ascribed to the light of the gospel shining in " darkness, which comprehended it not"—or to the influence of sound and cultivated reason—for reason and religion have the same objects. They are in no one instance opposed to each other. On the contrary, reason is nothing but imperfect religion, and religion is nothing but perfect reason.

It becomes christians to beware how far they condemn

the popular virtue of humanity, becaufe it is recommend-
ed by deiſts, or by perfons who do not profefs to be bound
by the ſtrict obligations of chriſtianity.—Voltaire firſt
taught the princes of Europe the duty of religious tolera-
tion. The duke of Sully has demonſtrated the extreme folly of war, and has proved that when it has been conducted
with the moſt glory, it never added an atom to national
happinefs. The marquis of Beccaria has eſtabliſhed a connexion between the abolition of capital puniſhments, and
the order and happinefs of fociety. Should any thing be
found in the ſcriptures, *contrary* to thefe difcoveries, it is
eafy to forefee that the principles of the deiſts and the laws
of modern legiſlators will foon have a *juſt* preference to the
principles and precepts of the gofpel.

Our author attempts to fupport his fanguinary tenets by
an appeal to revelation. And here I ſhall make two preli-
minary remarks.

1. There is no opinion fo abfurd or impious, that may
not be fupported by *folitary* texts of fcripture. To colled the
fenfe of the bible upon any fubject, we muſt be governed by
its *whole* fpirit and tenor.

2. The defign of chriſtianity at its firſt promulgation
was to reform the world by its *fpirit* rather than by its poſi-
tive precepts.

Our Saviour does not forbid flavery in direct terms—
but he indirectly bears a teſtimony againſt it, by command-
ing us to do to others what we would have them in like cir-
cumſtances to do to us. He did not aim to produce a fudden
revolution in the affairs of men. He knew too well the
power and efficacy of his religion for that purpofe. It was
unneceflary, therefore, to fubject it to additional oppoſi-
tion, by a direct attack upon the prejudices and intereſts of
mankind, both of which were clofely interwoven with the
texture of their civil governments.

After thefe remarks, I ſhall only add, that the declaration of St. Paul before Feſtus, refpecting the puniſhment
of death* and the fpeech of the dying thief on the crofs†,
only prove that the puniſhment of death was agreeable to
the Roman law, but they by no means prove that they
were fanctioned by the gofpel.—Human life was extremely

---

* " For if I be an offender, and have committed any
thing worthy of death, I refufe not to die." Acts 25 and 11.

† " We indeed" fuffer " *juſtly*, for we receive the due
" reward of our deeds." Luke 23 and 41.

cheap under the Roman government. Of this we need no further proof than the head of John the baptift forming a part of a royal entertainment. From the frequency of public executions, among thofe people, the *fword* was confidered as an emblem of public juftice—but to fuppofe from this appeal to a fign of juftice, or from our Saviour's parable of the deftruction of the hufbandmen, that capital punifhments are approved of in the new teftament, is as abfurd as it would be to fuppofe that horferacing was a chriftian exercife, from St. Paul's frequent allufions to the Olympic games.

The declaration of the barbarians upon feeing the fnake faften upon St. Paul's hand proves nothing but the ignorance of thofe uncivilized people. I deny the confent of all nations to the punifhment of death for murder—but if it were true—it only proves the univerfality of the ignorance and depravity of man. Revenge, diffimulation, and even theft, prevail among all the nations in the world,—and yet who will dare to affert, that thefe vices are juft, or neceffary to the order or happinefs of fociety.

Our author does not diftinguifh between the fenfe of juftice fo univerfal among all nations, and an approbation of death as a punifhment for murder. The former is written by the finger of God upon every human heart, but like his own attribute of juftice, it has the happinefs of individuals and of fociety for its objects. It is always mifled, when it feeks for fatisfaction in punifhments that are injurious to fociety, or that are difproportioned to crimes. The fatisfaction of this univerfal fenfe of juftice by the punifhments of imprifonment and labour, would far exceed that which is derived from the punifhment of death ; for it would be of longer duration, and it would more frequently occur, for, upon a principle laid down in the firft effay upon this fubject, fcarcely any fpecies of murder would efcape with impunity.*

---

* A fcale of punifhments by means of imprifonment and labour might eafily be contrived, fo as to be accommodated to the different degrees of atrocity in murder. For example—for the firft or higheft degree of guilt, let the punifhment be folitude and darknefs, and a total *want* of employment. For the fecond, folitude and labour, with the benefit of light. For the third, confinement and labour. The *duration* of thefe punifhments fhould likewife be governed by the atrocity of the murder, and by the figns of contrition and amendment in the criminal.

The conduct and discourses of our Saviour should out-weigh every argument that has been or can be offered in favour of capital punishment for any crime. When the wo-man caught in adultery was brought to him, he evaded in-flicting the bloody sentence of the Jewish law upon her. Even the *maiming* of the body appears to be offensive in his sight, for when Peter drew his sword and smote off the ear of the servant of the high priest, he replaced it by miracle, and at the same time declared, that "all they who take the sword, shall perish with the sword." He for-gave the crime of murder, on his cross ; and after his resur-rection, he commanded his disciples to preach the gospel of forgiveness *first* at Jerusalem, where he well knew his murderers still resided. These striking facts are recorded for our imitation, and seem intended to show that the Son of God died, not only to reconcile God to man, but to re-concile men to each other. There is one passage more, in the history of our Saviour's life, which would of itself overset the justice of the punishment of death for murder, if every other part of the bible had been silent upon the subject. When two of his disciples, actuated by the spirit of vindictive legislators, requested permission of him to call down fire from heaven to consume the inhospitable Sama-ritans, he answered them "the Son of man is not come to *destroy* men's *lives*, but to *save* them." I wish these words composed the motto of the arms of every nation upon the face of the earth. They inculcate every duty that is calculat-ed to preserve—restore—or prolong human life. They mili-tate alike against war—and capital punishments—the objects of which are the unprofitable destruction of the lives of men. How precious does a human life appear from these words, in the sight of heaven ! Pause, legislators, when you give your votes for inflicting the punishment of death for any crime. You frustrate, in one instance, the design of the mission of the Son of God into the world, and thereby either deny his appearance in the flesh, or reject the truth of his gospel. You moreover strengthen by your conduct the ar-guments of the deists and socinians against the particular doctrines of the christian revelation. You do more—you pre-serve a bloody fragment of the Jewish institution. "The Son of man came not to *destroy* men's lives, but to *save* them." Excellent words ! I require no others to satisfy me of the truth and divine original of the christian religion, and while I am able to place a finger upon this text of scripture, I will not believe an angel from heaven, should he declare that the punifhment of death for *any* crime was inculcated, or permitted by the fpirit of the gofpel.

It has been faid, that a man who has committed a murder, has difcovered a malignity of heart, that renders him ever afterwards unfit to live in human fociety. This is by no means true in many, and perhaps in moft of the cafes of murder. It is moft frequently the effect of a fudden guft of paffion, and has fometimes been the only ftain of a well fpent or inoffenfive life. There are many crimes which unfit a man much more for human fociety, than a fingle murder, and there have been inftances of murderers who have efcaped or bribed the laws of their country, who have afterwards become peaceable, and ufeful members of fociety. Let it not be fuppofed that I wifh to palliate by this remark, the enormity of murder. Far from it. It is only becaufe I view murder with fuch fuperlative horror, that I wifh to deprive our laws of the power of perpetrating and encouraging it.

Our author has furnifhed us with a number of tales to fhow that the providence of God is concerned in a peculiar manner in detecting murder, and that the confeffions of murderers have in many inftances fanctified the juftice of their punifhment. I do not wifh to leffen the influence of fuch vulgar errors as tend to prevent crimes, but I will venture to declare, that many more murderers efcape difcovery, than are detected, or punifhed. Were I not afraid of trefpaffing upon the patience of my readers, I might mention a number of facts, in which circumftances of the moft trifling nature have become the means of detecting theft and forgery, from which I could draw as ftrong proofs of the watchfulnefs of providence over the property of individuals, and the order of fociety, as our author has drawn from the detection of murder. I might mention inftances, likewife, of perfons in whom confcience has produced reftitution for ftolen goods, or confeffion of the juftice of the punifhment which was inflicted for theft. Confcience and knowledge always keep pace with each other, both with refpect to divine and human laws. A party of foldiers in the duke of Alva's army, murdered a man and his wife with fix children. They roafted the youngeft child, and dined upon it. One of them after dinner clapped his hands together, and with great agitation of mind cried out " good God—what have I done ?"—What ? faid one of his companions—" why" faid the other " I have eaten flefh in lent time." Here confcience kept pace with his degrees of knowledge. The fame thing occurs upon different occafions

every day. The acquiefcence of murderers in the juftice
of their execution, is the effect of prejudice and education.
It cannot flow from a confcience acting in concert with
reafon or religion—for they both fpeak a very different
language.

The world has certainly undergone a material change
for the better within the laft two hundred years. This
change has been produced chiefly, by the fecret and un-
acknowledged influence of chriftianity upon the hearts of
men. It is agreeable to trace the effects of the chriftian religion in the extirpation of flavery—in the diminution of
the number of capital punifhments, and in the mitigation
of the horrors of war. There was a time when mafters pof-
feffed a power over the lives of their flaves. But chriftianity
has depofed this power, and mankind begin to fee every
where that flavery is alike contrary to the interefts of fociety, and the fpirit of the gofpel. There was a time when tor-
ture was part of the punifhment of death, and when the
number of capital crimes amounted to one hundred and fix-
ty-one. Chriftianity has abolifhed the former, and reduced
the latter to not more than fix or feven. It has done more.
It has confined in fome inftances capital punifhments to the
crime of murder only—and in fome countries it has abolifhed it altogether. The influence of chriftianity upon the
modes of war has been ftill more remarkable. It is agreeable to trace its progrefs.

1ft. In refcuing women and children from being the objects of the defolations of war in common with men.

2dly. In preventing the deftruction of captives taken in
battle, in cold blood.

3dly. In protecting the peaceable hufbandman from fhar-
ing in the carnage of war.

4thly. In producing an exchange of prifoners, inftead of
dooming them to perpetual flavery.

5thly. In avoiding the invafion or deftruction, in certain
cafes, of private property.

6thly. In declaring all wars to be unlawful but fuch as
are purely *defenfive*.

This is the only tenure by which war now holds its place
among chriftians. It requires but little ingenuity to prove
that a defenfive war cannot be carried on fuccefsfully without
offenfive operations. If this be true, then this laft degree of
it, upon our author's principles, muft be contrary to the
fpirit of the gofpel. Already the princes and nations of the
world difcover the ftruggles of opinion or confcience is

C

their preparations for war. Witnefs, the many national difputes which have been lately terminated in Europe by negociation, or mediation. Witnefs, too, the eftablifhment of the conftitution of the united ftates without force or bloodfhed. Thefe events indicate an improving ftate of human affairs. They lead us to look forward with expectation to the time, when the weapons of war fhall be changed into implements of hufbandry, and when rapine and violence fhall be no more. Thefe events are the promifed fruits of the gofpel. If they do not come to pafs, the prophets have deceived us. But if they do—war muft be as contrary to the fpirit of the gofpel, as fraud, or murder, or any other of the vices which are reproved or extirpated by it*.

I cannot take leave of this fubject without remarking that capital punifhments are the natural offspring of monarchical governments. Kings believe that they pofefs their crowns by a *divine* right: no wonder, therefore, they affume the divine power of taking away human life. Kings confider their fubjects as their property : no wonder, therefore, they fhed their blood with as little emotion as men fhed the blood of their fheep or cattle. But the principles of republican governments fpeak a very different language. They teach us the abfurdity of the divine origin of kingly power. They approximate the extreme ranks of men to each other. They reftore man to his God—to fociety— and to himfelf. They revive and eftablifh the relations of fellow-citizen, friend, and brother. They appreciate human life, and increafe public and private obligations to preferve it. They confider human facrifices as no lefs offenfive to the fovereignty of the people, than they are to the majefty of heaven. They view the attributes of government, like the attri   of the deity, as infinitely more honoured by deftroying evil by means of *merciful* than by exterminating punifhments. The united ftates have adopted thefe peaceful and benevolent forms of government. It becomes them therefore to adopt their mild and benevolent

---

* The fpirit of chriftianity which our author defcribey as a vulgar deiftical fpecies of humanity, has found its was into fchools and families, and has abolifhed, in both, corporal and ignominious punifhments. In the inftructions to the mafters and miftrefles of the fundry fchools, I obferve with great pleafure a direction " to ufe corporal punifhments as feldom as poffible."

principles. An execution in a republic is like a human facrifice in religion. It is an offering to monarchy, and to
that malignant being, who has been ftiled a murderer from
the beginning, and who delights equally in murder, whether it be perpetrated by the cold, but vindictive arm of
the law, or by the angry hand of private revenge.

T H E E N D.

www.ingramcontent.com/pod-product-compliance
Lightning Source LLC
Chambersburg PA
CBHW031159090426
42738CB00008B/1392